Praise for *The Orchestra of Wind Chimes*

"'What happened to the beautiful language?' asks Geoffrey Jacques's opening line of *The Orchestra of Wind Chimes*. The answer is it is here in poem after poem of his new collection containing clean, clear, compressed, meditative, and intuitive lines that will leave a haunting sensation lingering on the periphery of your mind."

—Bill Harris, 2011 Kresge Foundation Eminent Artist

"*A Change in the Weather, Just for a Thrill*, Geoffrey Jacques has always been attentive to what was in the wind but was never one simply to look at the wind sock and follow the drift. His has always been a writing on the storm, a writing at the edge of night. And now his *The Orchestra of Wind Chimes* is tolling our times."

—Aldon Nielsen

"*The Orchestra of Wind Chimes* by Geoffrey Jacques never captivates by hardening itself into the province of fatigue but susurrates according to grammar by moonlight and never presents itself according to the isolated folly that is day-to-day captivation."

—Will Alexander

The Orchestra of Wind Chimes

Made in Michigan Writers Series

GENERAL EDITORS

Michael Delp, Interlochen Center for the Arts
M. L. Liebler, Wayne State University

A complete listing of the books in this series can be
found online at wsupress.wayne.edu.

The Orchestra of Wind Chimes

POEMS BY GEOFFREY JACQUES

WAYNE STATE UNIVERSITY PRESS
DETROIT

ISBN 9780814350386 (paperback)
ISBN 9780814350393 (e-book)

Library of Congress Control Number: 2022945066

Publication of this book was made possible by a generous gift from The Meijer Foundation.

Cover image © Stocksy/Marcos Osorio. Cover design by Laura Klynstra.

Wayne State University Press rests on Waawiyaataanong, also referred to as Detroit, the ancestral and contemporary homeland of the Three Fires Confederacy. These sovereign lands were granted by the Ojibwe, Odawa, Potawatomi, and Wyandot nations, in 1807, through the Treaty of Detroit. Wayne State University Press affirms Indigenous sovereignty and honors all tribes with a connection to Detroit. With our Native neighbors, the press works to advance educational equity and promote a better future for the earth and all people.

Wayne State University Press
Leonard N. Simons Building
4809 Woodward Avenue
Detroit, Michigan 48201-1309

Visit us online at wsupress.wayne.edu.

For Sherri

CONTENTS

III

IV

ACKNOWLEDGMENTS

Grateful acknowledgment is made to the editors of the following publications and websites, where some of the poems in this book first appeared:

Askew: "How"

Black Renaissance Noire: "Extravaganzas," "Ode," "Rhetorical Questions," "The Cilantro of Generals," "What Comes Between Them," "Pillarless," "Quality Phase," "Erector Set," and "Sentimental Education"

Fence: "Delaware Water Gap" and "Letter"

Live Mag: "Exemplar" and "Hymn"

MiPOesias: "Watch," "A Settling Storm," "Proposition," and "Knowledge Wakes You Up: What Does That Tell You?"

Miramar: "Plenty"

O-Blek: "Ars Poetica"

phati'tude: "I Heard All the Music as If They Were Drums"

Ping-Pong, An Art and Literary Journal of the Henry Miller Library: "That in the Ayre doth lome"

Sharing with Lindamichelle Baron (http://lindamichellebaron.com/): "The Calculus of Acceptable Sins" and "Ray Charles"

Tidal Basin Review: "Of Identity," "Detour Ahead"

Vanitas: "July Nights," "Empty Pockets," and "Mating Call"

I

Viewers Like

what happened to the beautiful language?
we pressed a button & wondered: such fun

against the white background
links to locked out pictures
the world's falling bridges

& other reminders of our neglect

they're just a substitute for noisy, expensive machines
whose comfort is flashy & colored
a name we now know, a meaning that's both friend & function

& whose preaching brings forth scattered—

Some Parts of It

The wind blows the curtains dance
& elsewhere another does too

& if you care that's news to me
they say there's rain let's dare some wicks

*

one thousand people lay dead in the street
live in your own neighborhood, for work & play

money shows up in every other line
the rain stopped most of us from wasting

& there's this addled bonus
you have time to do nothing

*

(Vocalion rhubarb alternates constructed dreams
don't give up! designer specialties get results

*

—I am dreaming of the sky
a voice predicts unseasonably warm weather
& look at the evening sun browning the harbor
& the cutest blond sparks a desire
to cross the border & drown in myth)

*

the old note falls silent
on the wind-swept streets

the clapboarded days
refuse the sun's winded shine
refuse to barter

frozen time, guilty
of its own green

Stopped Here Momentarily for an Indefinite Period

already raging much earlier & faster
buttermilk complete, spinned out & clearly excited

get the facts: call this number, see how you'll be connected
the principal group—huh? I can't hear you, sticks together

this should really help as we move through the morning hours
it's the taste everybody will love; I'm a little bit of luck

Still Life

produces this delectable creature
made to live in a delicate network

to feed en masse on the sun-drenched drying limbs
under the darkening heavy sky

the word, complex as this old factory
resists inscription, defers light

feeds like insects at labor, busily
reveals only its mask, masked

Of

—as if in answer, the blade, alone & unafraid
gives nothing of itself, nothing but—

elsewhere the effort & its illusions

& the hands that realize are honored only in the glass
here, under the whispering wind, in repose

The Calculus of Acceptable Sins

Half the night I've sat up reading & fearing the mosquito
that buzzed in my ear a while ago

it landed on the wall, then haunted the edge of my sight

I broke a book trying to smash it
knowing what will happen when the room finally goes dark

*

I am sorry that my phonemes threaten your sinecure
I am sorry that my manners threaten your poverty
I am sorry that my language scares your cover
I am sorry that my identity threatens your identity

*

all day long the heat has promised to invade my chamber
against it I deploy many weapons: fans in every room
an attitude of indifference, a reverence for the green outside these
    walls—

& with the night the cricket chirps
a reminder that we are all servants of mercy

*

A wasp flutters first on one doorway's side & now on the other
before speeding toward the woods on its own business

early summer trees at attention
the painted walkway—bright with the sun's brushwork
is full of shadows, too

& here I sit with my own thoughts
lost in sound awash in the leafy day

Has Happened

. . . dysphoric plausibility argues obsessive suffering
where ambiguity serves forms of control
& address recuperates tensions, making a case for translation

cross-culture analogies & codes assert private travelogues

the legal restrictions entertain agency
contradiction posits insistent feelings

but pressures broaden discourse
demonstrations impress spatial tradition
& context accomplishes textuality

the idea preoccupies or defends contemporary experience
stories mark bodies difficult words cohere
meditation crosses intention unreliable witnesses testify

her problem? silence & bad morale
violent texts represent advocacy

Nelson Rockefeller Sees Lenin

& art: integrity & fees
& the public means comics

saints resolve their differences, harshly
blasting at the walls

a destroyed work "packed with energy & ideas"

& way back there, the syphilitic tormenter
but here's how the big town might have gone: work as spirit
   & art form

The Echo's Nadir

At the horizon the fog saturates the bridges, the statues,
the quiet smokestacks & the amplification in the wet air

beyond, in the shade, someone is crying
& last night, approaching the door, the sounds of two feet
punctuating the moonlight concluded the tale

Myopia

There must be a way to put this simply
suddenly that afternoon all the sounds ceased
the twilight winds the small talk of the dead
the barren tree in its statuesque pose
& from across the dust-covered yard you face both lovers

a garbled tongue with its pristine hue
& a cup from someplace nestling in a chair

Chance It

if I were you I'd just skip the light fandango
& wang dang doodle till the cows came home

let your backbone slip
& let your ding-dong daddy from Dumas
be your butter & egg man

that's what I'd do if I were you
& forget about the rest of this trash

Amulet

Your eyes staring like smoldering roses
your oval mouth fixed in concentrated pleasure
the small cries from your throat's mysterious catacombs
joining the orchestra of wind chimes & rattling window-panes

—he'd planned a different rendezvous
a meeting with friends in a small gray city
it was to be made festive: together they would launch the grand effort
the gesture required of old hands—

ah . . . to sink deeper into this warm moisture
listening to muffled laughter nuzzling my ear
—a laughter that assassinates winter—
as my hands roam across your smooth chocolate skin

July Nights

They stream through the drowsy leaves
these slight night sounds

—the fan, the air conditioner
young men at the corner long since used to darkness

there should be beautiful & strangely colored acts to imagine here
the lights across the courtyard
burn in the vacant chamber
& in the stifling air, a woman sings

"That in the Ayre doth lome"
—Thomas Wyatt

—take your clothes off
night through sheer curtains
still wind, clear moon
& from the glass by the bed, a glint—

*

& here your arms
bathed in glowing
these relations, the gamble

sweet sandwiches, the voyage
discrete night
joy of the same bird
"whoop" through the screen

*

yes, remove this distraction
we'll bask in the bells
in the expectant light
in that breath-deep call
in that dusty fragrance

II

The Problem of Speech Genres

what was said was only a scrap
that flag fluttering in midsummer is not conjure's feeling
a model held against aching nostalgia
can merely be understood one angle at a time

—or listen to that wail trailing off into the city's depths—
what broken bones heaped on a steamy bed
hide within the ambulette rushing below
—string them together & hold them up to the light—

you heard the fragment passing by
& stood there wondering as we all did

but it fits right where it's always been
—in the middle, otherwise it would
continue namelessly along—

*

window stares at window
which in turn stares
at the transparency across the way

nothing else is visible: not hearer not this low chattering
these incongruous conceits which just might make the evening news
or this pair of dispassionately upturned lips

*

a pair of wrens mating on the sunlit wire
is perhaps a fragment awaiting its context
but I worry about my friend
missing & late for our rendezvous

each whim exists—the scribe whispers—
in reflection or anticipation
as the day gets hotter then cooler
—make of it what you will—
but at a crucial point in the drama
one hurls itself straight toward the concrete
dropping about ten feet through the air
before speeding swiftly eastward
leaving its partner alone in the yellow breeze

Ars Poetica

*"when you hear music after it's over
it's gone
in the air
you can never
capture it again"*

—Eric Dolphy

I don't know why all the rules should suddenly go topsy-turvy
& the half-century old standard with its great flakes
& impossibly svelte & desirable ikons
go unheeded as we consider raising one piece against another

in our never-ending search for significance in the fine print
where—just as luck would have it—
only a precious few can get any real satisfaction
as they leave us alone to fend for ourselves

Proposition

unlike the leaves lost to the night
those shouts along the sun-speckled canals
the dripping piercing potted wall
—*this is important*: unlike the raisin-studded afternoon
these side streets polished with horsehair brushes—my heart—

the palace of justice blockaded by pacifists
the steep rattling midnight stairway
the headless cough seeping through a sea-green chasm
the ubiquitous mysterious triplet crosses

—the commonsense thing is to say "it's normal"
just one foot in front of the other like a gazelle—

but they were heard somewhere
these shifts in your breathing
the directionless movement was a sign

Letter

Far away longing & life's competitive claims
like the unthinkable poet-in-German
we desire what appears in cold clouds & water
clinging to an afternoon-in-transit

to know what to do or how to do it
to avoid interference to hold on despite hearing nothing

Today's colliding winds buffet oncoming traffic
I've forgotten little for a change & believe even less
But there's this: no, there's the blank page moving in with the sky

A Figurative Novella

You want to hand over some old jewels
but I don't know what they mean
I don't know about the loves lost before you could speak

—the sunny afternoons
the sweltering idling car—

& life's mysteries still flutter around
like a butterfly's disemboweled wings
—brightly colored but vapid—

The Cilantro of Generals

Americans to market driven,
And bartered as the brute for gold!
—J. G. Whittier,
"Expostulation"
(1834)

Mercantile drovers & no added sugar
asks you to mate with a sprig while he has sexual
mistaken for shady unsuspecting town folk

the term "field grade" is for Colonels & Generals
the distinctively fresh taste: sports
discover blatant irregularities in ale

world domination chemically speaking
is an interesting petition
the ongoing synergy between big & small

gemstone gendarme gendered generals generate generics generous
to Abydos: "you'll have to share," then slip along
who moved during the 8th century?

break for breakfast of pho
& takes Gam & her nieces
two hours to arrange the fabrics

absolutely must please the generals
ministers girlfriends bosses
& yet believe in the military the war machine

& do not diet & chunks of tough
& home century being alive
& one billion to slow Africa

about "necessary" evil: the trouble *is* Dostum
this October celebrate the popular
the destruction is commissioned

boot camp buddies support this forum
post a new topic for my profile: cellophane
they're anointed, money, in order to protect

these planes are threatening our cities
—please have them noodled—
a lot better with a touch at ten-for-a-dollar

Kurfürsten Damm

They say it's the biggest military operation since
you'll find no politics here, my friend
all the crackling murmurs the fast cars
the double decker buses the satisfaction

besides, that was all so long ago
it's May! & the fighting is elsewhere
as Sam Cooke used to sing, Oh! way back when

& a couple skates past the spot
where cops in flak jackets
just a moment ago
stood drinking mineral water

Crossing Delaware Water Gap

the coat's margin is style's limit
he woke up that once more last
& shook his shags & growled

shiny shenanigans crowd the rigged ice
blue in the creamy afternoon's brownish flickerby
ridge of spiky wood-dried stand at attention
who can't believe light's sole property

this breezeless warren of purposeless pleasure
this pair of white vans made for titillations
the third pond the day's concupiscence
past the abandoned magnificent cranes

O bridges & clapboard & gray winged critters
that portico beneath the flag pointed north

Extravaganzas

Music is inherently psychedelic
—Tan Lin

—who wishes to aid the global trance movement
this isn't really a survey, because it doesn't strange
start breaking my heart! & buy this now
who believes the spiritual in the mundane

the act will have shown the nature of traditional forms
& equally flawed & thrust into imagining
a stunning tapestry swirls: unabashedly impassioned melancholic
decimation, breakdown, reformation, purging

on Saturdays, play oriental, play surf, like grease
because the installation is simple but the mainstream
pranksters made drugs & what makes them so different
is a brand of angst rehashing garage dictation

aural stimulus: then sure, baby, there's a political dimension
it's something odd, seeming nonsense, fascinating
furthermore the light at each experience individualized
to describe religious elements without resorting

on ecstasy on white rabbit on sometimes subversive
on being moved on artificial facsimile on especially
to eat on mental residue on pop of down on through the explosive
on the most enduring on the one most tasty

my favorite events: past, presented, delightful, stunning
blow themselves up, gives others this same experience
& there's the aspect to bit smart sound click
though he has since moved on to what seems to be a phase

but more commonly, means project the existing self-illusion
classic & prayerful from the world of marks
"nice weather for ducks" & most importantly, uplifting
as a tribute to something disrespectful

with its mix of exuberant analog bombast
that recalls furs, & glass & orange mountain
the problem that permeates is simple
say it all feels much more American

enthusiasm corporate setting thumping stirringly emotional
creates exquisite thinking & toughens the mercury
even doctoring, lawyering or legislating
as though there was something wrong with that—

Refinement

The words you overhear
are like the machines of a warm night
they substitute for silence
for the color of solitude

are they words of love gone sour
once heard in a distant city
where a boy consoles his brother
with a sound whose meaning is obscure?

what is obscure: sirens of a terror that arrived later
after they were silenced by our confidence

that now appears as cancer & headache & toothache
& cough & the overdosed dead & the drawn clouded faces

a terror lived in relative luxury
a vanishing point
blue like fluttering water

Knowledge Wakes You Up: What Does That Tell You?

the moon drops eerily into the sea-soaked sky
the seagulls are not friendly

it's relaxing: dry green
cries along shrouded cliffs
the steps end at the crucifixed border

& that structure? a position was a shelter
now a dump made orange by wind
made over by droppings
not unlike our now-fabled moon

*

—the plane dives toward the sun
its shadow prances among waves

beneath the citrus coverlet
along the sheer cliffs
in the mouth of the soft sea
—teach the kitchen parrot
to say fuck you in 3 languages—
"the reward of that agonizing difference
for all its concretion precision oneness
is desperately difficult to communicate"

get your face gussied up
& stroll along the strand
the signs bordering our movements

*

say: snoring through plaster
"this blazing white, unchanging respite"
flanks the gritty closed shutters
held against the double-breasted tide
its salty crustaceous vapors
its echoing footsteps

alongside the azure-bathed dock
the unremembered ideal
Hollywood-style horror picture houses
—yellow ballast black body-suited surfers
empty water bottles—
pale plaster debris escapes
—& just east of the afternoon green
what passes, these days, for the new—

*

& the "sensuous concrete"
& the rising white birds who've stopped feeding on nature
now on our turf in our sandbox
collect pretty shells
& use them to ignite dreams

*

& you've come back after so many years
the morning gulls dance above the harbor
the fickle sun visits sails at rest
flickers in your hair your shining grass eyes

—to worry about names or the continuing tale is useless
we're not sitting among blue verses
your nasal dreams like sea-painted pebbles
& the plain bread of this country—

Mating Call

—the streets shine like electric tar like licorice
each store I pass, looking for old goods in new packaging
evaporates commercial desire

at dinner I stare at a pretty face
she doesn't stare back

the bread is chewy the wine bitter

in an East Village bookstore a grey-haired man
instructs his young companion
all the way home I constantly think in numbers
of how much I hate working overtime—

Empty Pockets

clear of the closing, we don't know
there, in the wing of silence, dull pixels

or on the wall, where once dreamed
"salute the spirit of perfection"

memory is its moment of abuse
"hope" the new brand recognition

& placement is all; placement rocks

One of the only points on a plane
one of the only tiny bottle caps
one of the only speckled specks
one of the only slabs of erotic linoleum
one of the only orphaned bells
one of the only dismembered skylights
one of the only arcs of neon
one of the only badly turned blondes
one of the only commodified water bottles
one of the only blurred blue signs
one of the only sheer stones
one of the only counts of yes
one of the only information parasites
one of the only inquiring architectures
one of the only careful entries
one of the only attacking snowbirds
one of the only gray beards looking
one of the only extinguished fezzes
one of the only fuzzy talks
one of the only rainy puzzles
one of the only disenchanted fickles

What Comes Between Them

Where there are clichés there are mountains
where there are mountains there are clichés

take these singing birds for instance
once in a while a plane drones overhead
& moss grows on the thatched roof a few feet away

okay, so it happens more often than that
even here, so near the wilderness
there are regular schedules

kept by those who, like this pair at sunrise
—the one who sings, the one who drones—
have no clue to the abyss in the midst of this idyll

*

in the sun all day reading poems
the black dog chasing geese
ripples spring from the powerboats
—the small talk of politics—

—easy for you to call it wisdom
to take for granted your own unhappiness

But the guy who grieves
is looking for just that heartache
to travel with down the road a piece

*

the yawn is just as big
only the pleasures—at least at first glance—
seem brighter if no cheaper

between desire & this faint echo
the panting the stifled cry—

*

one thing fills this gap: silence
not silence exactly: the echo of plumbing
those sighs I hear through the wall
the pregnant sleep of birds

& not even—strictly speaking—a gap
those who envy his choices
what do they know? who disbelieve your restrictive space
the adept who's deaf to local languages

*

a traveler is but (sigh) even the old poem's phrase
heard too often is itself paltry
worn as this light is worn

a sheet over which clouds roll west

*

& no you can't dress for it
just let the chills arrive
on the repast's heels

tonight you'll catch one more dream
the sort that seems at home here
under the green & gray
under the droning canopy

Rhetorical Questions

*

(how you could know the ear
its resonance among stones
in the dewy evening
an evening the light glutted
spun in its own mist
its garland shorn

& if it still feels untried
consider the grammar
of waiting of surrender)

1

raunchy: that's the way of adults, ain't it?
I mean: "2 masters one book" can be more than
a pix in a tunnel the announcer's glib newsstand
more than "solar" broken in the middle against the window

—whew, that's a relief
nothing like a word to get started—

It's true that we're ruled by ignorance?
don't ask with golden leaves in the vortex
it'll ruin pleasant reveries

2

offer as a supposition only
—was he talking about you?
American parents spend thousands
but the anxious election was nixed

trembling, as he did, while passing Canal

if the associations are lost don't get up
it's just one more brand you're wearing
a signal to broadcast belonging
a sign of officially mediated rebellion

*

(alone, coverlets mute in the dim yellow light
a chance (perhaps) not yet forsaken

noises rudely awaken
a silence escaping

if memory speaks
if memory stings

one voice that begs forgiveness
that begs—at last—for its chorus)

Ode

facilitate core cross-functions
share your life with knowledge
think over the performance
pursue an open synergy

embrace smart excellence
enhance global content

utilize this capital position
to mean effective growth

make the product foster information
for instance: market as system
above sound as solution

*

the imagination has always been
an independent country

*

interactive technology is the cost
& synergistic partners form multitaskical value

so communicate high futures

create an objectively hot decision

*

meet us in an emerged business
& feel a team-based vision
an intensive organization

a professionally built economy must know
that the network intermatched
yet some problem competed
to manage & identify his bold mission

I Heard All the Music as If They Were Drums

In memory of James Brown

I got to be concerned
I got to paint it real
someone shot the guy in the back who wanted—

my music was becoming overtly political
it became real with the white & colored water fountains

politics had done nothing for them
he was a dropout, you might as well be dead
I never had a chance, I was taken by the authorities

do what you got to do as a people—
I always said that, do it all the time

he gives them bicycles, he doesn't forget where he comes from

Sweet says, behind closed doors
right here, whatever you do won't be right
the only thing you have to rely on is your memory
that's been with him have been with him for many years
get up get on up get up get on up get up get on up get up—

he enjoyed himself, he became angry I don't understand what that
    anger was

a lot of strange things were happening
the whole country was up in flames
I can't believe the system: so man, relax

there were hundreds of fires hundreds of arrests
I told the police to back off
you want to dance? then dance

I can't stand it, babe, look a' here—

he was not going by their permission
I didn't go to Vietnam to fight: the music was so loud there was a cease-fire
    while I was on stage

—I was a teenager at the time & in many ways he was—

it was a song to uplift black people: say it loud, birds & bees
"we'd rather die on our feet than be livin' on our knees"

I wasn't mad at nobody
identity was up for grabs

(then there's the gold platter)

I was just buying opportunity
I took my music where it belonged
to the ghettos & the prisons

what I heard was the jingle jangle of a thousand lost souls

Pillarless

It's called what, study in England
psychoanalysis takes into account
it's not the world that's disappointed me
or gives decadent societies the noise
or bluntly wants to be convinced

keep yourself in the background & remember market honor
circle words or notes, consult birds
plots that work conflict with the real world
unsuccessful attempts between three ways to mambo

use your own Dow to create experience
proper time, truck devastation, took the matter personally
each comprised no more than the same pattern

Quality Phase

complete autonomy makes jade & white thoughts
shed standards with far less power
they're all under transferals
"rather low by our lights" & "we fart on what they're going to do"
this spread across centuries & left for dead
& wondering what to do with the money

Grandale is a one-hour or one-half-hour sample
applying inadequate tape involved in local effects

but you didn't even listen, imagine that!
so the guy feels left out of the deal:
214 applications; 18 funded; 7 people on the panel;
it's all you can do to just keep calm with all these voices
sated limericks, steep horizons: would she go for it?
that's unlikely in this state of wonder

Erector Set

confidence lit & wandering
raw clove sun, evaporated sober money
push down & turn: burgundy estrella connects the fine requirements
& next to the very first smoked terrine
is the dynamic rhinestone

to avoid danger? take a hike & keep out blowback

(how dense not to know the best poet in America
pursue this if you want to: behind toast
pick the time & place, *no doubt*)

an opportunity plan creates or saves
it's one of the greatest ironies in shopping
when you get angry go to stereotype
a worthless, bankrupt, single vision

"abstraction has not been critiqued"
but I came to it thinking about culture
reductionist confinement, completely covered by narrative
architectural ideas connect to content
& allow thinking to go outside itself

a burdensome discourse
imprisoned by reference
bounded by history

disconnected identities associated with poverty

so what? ghetto voices in suburban homes
like a minstrel jacked "out of time"
(such hunger to be accepted such crazy ends)
or that bright cloth flapping in the wind
its colors jangling, a dappled voice

Of Identity

—thank the beginning, the foundation of the unwanted—

then there are those powered by "Roots," & evening serials
that's what educated them: not the war, not the noise, not ideas, not
    vision

yet with a clear or opaque chronicle, if you spend time there
you'll find different, creepy, contemplative things
—know the vehicle as color, that's one idea of time—
weighted on top of another, like an umber façade

on the other hand, again concerning color, as part of nature itself

it need not be apparent
does not have to be monstrous

it can be the side of the eye

Ray Charles

Crushed icicles the heaving & panting are only a beginning
formerly we waved our flags wherever we went
now we abandon our hearts to loveless love
our excuses laid bare before the court

remember that tall tale about the one who waited for you
at the other end of this sleepy city
while in the background a wordless picture
love perhaps or a poor reflection
conjured an image of smoke & the bad air
that being too near in the wrong place
late at night can bring to the careless

it's old, an old yarn I tell you
but we enjoy it anyway
even though we know better
even though we know that in the end
bright eyes mirror stars of ribboned desire

Detour Ahead

a differently valued official ideology pursues performance
though history & biography ponder sexuality

—the intimate mode framed
by a market-arranged relation—

pedagogy without looking
conditional not consequent
a different kind of work
the sticky of sticky face

only in America did I learn
what it means to be a person of color

& the rupture within that meaning
a thing deeply amenable to the foul interplay of language
resist: image-making underground
a text in multiple locations

the opportunity in a group
will mistake the personnel director
a categorically imperative ecology

when A stands for what B represents
paranoia stands in for personal essay

our obsession is a lot like penetration
a normalizing action across a table

composition & marginalization
the full-fledged underrated stepchild
—egalitarian popular roots—
involves knowing the system will be allowed to evaporate

the attack has been so scurrilous
battling on your own turf
broodily blowing the lid

non-dualisms break the taboo
the division of labor the paradigm

people become traffic—fill in the blank—

an intervention will encourage the range of who's in the rolodex
but what happens depends on what's asked

IV

A Wit of Cackle

imagine my marked distaste as I squinted
comparing a lounge to a cooked discharge

it wasn't comfortable, yet no one had the guts to hurry up & reign in
  my trouble

the appeal was broken, a thoughtful reflex omitted the implied, if
  grand embrace

& the unutterable, tough ridicule that's sure to come my way
with its robe carved with nicknames
its kindred, gummy dazzle
& its brown & yellow perch

is just a congruent fog, a wit of cackle

two golden-winged butterflies run after each other through the bush
an unseen cry hovering about, pointedly sharp

clear light, ringing bell, gentle fountain
a faraway gadget's roar, a dancing fern

in the heated wind little gnats flitter
while beyond the door, the abrupt quiet
like the wind wheel not far away

& the long shadow creased with pale yellow
framing the mild nap of the day, its dippy container
its annoying talk, its coy etiquette

The Divergent

on the edge, where the big-winged raven lapping at the fountain

where a many-domed light is a premium estate
objectively honeyed, excellent return

& the relative position of wing to water
maker of the game, the bark, yellow-brown against the lively tableau
a poked beginning, like a gesture in a fairy tale

"Here's proof that there's no job shortage"
—email spam

Will require an optimized point across properties
to program banners, retarget, consult, guide, market

for an intake outfit looking for temporary work
must have done time, preferably in consumption

associates will monitor compliance: this individual will support
    compliance
in matters like rule, test, verification, adequacy, effectiveness
& affix the entry level pep talk if you sign up now

enjoy knowing the answer to people's questions? learn policies &
    procedures
cater new accounts & existing tactical profitability functions

—enter the challenge, reward domestic low-income protection
custody visitation, outting the league, in a bilingual relief—

*

when your disaster attorney was formed
representing people turned by appeals
an industry leader in livery
grew like weeds into the biggest garment

for support in preparing & filing
communications, keeper of trans trust
hit the Klondike, work overtime from home
we value your experience with debt

*

for a private acquisition of all aspects, practical leverage
& your integrated technical dynamic, consider malpractice

the strategic oversight candidate will activate a complex exposure
reflecting another broad category managing the craft over time

by loyally renewing a highly-developed focus on our merchandise

Hymn

for Amiri Baraka

much of it is cliché, an impractical turn
the naked ladies in the garden
& rarely here, an unbalanced view

& when I give over to the feeling
—just to mellow the edge—
you take my breath away

we all saw it coming, "that late death"
but the doubletalk? a crumbling walnut
fuzzy like a worn blue potholder

a tiny bird feeds, white bud to white bud
each palm branch dancing in the temperate light
next door, man & machine jar the tableau

& if our judge, the wind, will permit contemplation
& if we're absolved, to forgive might be golden

Nature Study

purple mountain's majesty
who'd dare use that phrase in a poem?
here cotton candy clouds wrench it from you
next right: the chrome blue future

over a quiet creek near Quebec
dry green is the moment's sign
walking at the concrete edge
near the continuous lake
flags flutter—no one knows why—
& the picture explodes, an eruption of light

Sonnet

for Wallace Stevens

the poppycock flayed the torrid mantle
watching a rotting palm tree as it fell
its rogue, brown, spiked leaves gaggle heartily
like a tinkling box behind the curtain

but wait & see: the racket up above
announced the early growth, the dull promise
of blue warmth, an incrementally wet
mortised billboard of camouflaged knowledge

while a high-&-mighty journey unfolds
rigged by a deflowered organism
the sun shines, the wind blows, the lilacs stare
as numb incubators fake delirium

& gripping the pot-bellied crap table
your rough doubling, like a bird, is braided

the upside-down water bottle could have led to disaster
that it didn't is not my fault

my only responsibility was to watch for hooligans
a job I did not fail to carry out

here now, as the light by turns
lets us know that no wire mistakenly crossed another
I can get rid of that nutty introjection

Oh, I'll continue to worry, even though
you might think the pay is oblique

& there we can find whatever they kept like new
puzzling at the oddly dim, uncertain reward

a figure behind a door of gauze

filling our ears like a rapid descent

A Note of Faint Praise

if you have the speech pattern, for example, of an endangered
   marigold

the constrained but hopeful purgative that typically vibrates along
   the path of empathy

& when you arrived like an embargoed retina delivered from luxury,
   glad to be in charge

the middle factor became available, a metronome of invocation

there, where the little dog stared out from your embrace
a damp road jolted ahead, guiding the whole field

but the puzzle intervened, like a marble plaything
& in your very own jack-in-the-box, a trick

I don't quite know what I'm doing
night sounds whoosh & whimper
Coleman Hawkins humming the moon
a lover anointed with plums

seasonal plaster & dirt draping each object like a cool giveaway
here a chair there a lamp a ratty couch
a fine carpet an altar to the slaughtered path

each mite gathering in every corner
the melody drifting away over the rooftops

The Subject of the Poem

cyborgs argue among themselves
climbing a wet lattice
—talk about medicine—

recycled from an applied reserve
the sensualist collects total losses
the lot is defined differently

dial wisdom for moisture
the unnatural index

your lecture on change is like a winged horse keyed to weather

between a spiritual native utopia
& that blue chant to the moon
measured breath, the way sound cracks

knowing the world generates favorites
& sparks unfinished commerce
a pod desperately learning timidity